AF433035

Seasons of the Soul

THE POET'S SONG

JOHN DAVID SMITH

Cover design by Elev8d Designs.

Scribe & Canvas Publishing
South Carolina

© 2024 John David Smith.
All rights reserved.

First Printing

The poems in this book are works of fiction and personal reflection. Any resemblance to real persons, living or dead, is purely coincidental and not intended by the author.

No part of this book may be reproduced, or stored in a retrieval system, or transmitted in any form or by any means, electronic, mechanical, photocopying, recording, or otherwise, without express written permission of the publisher.

Paperback 979-8-3484-2209-7

Published by Scribe & Canvas Publishing™
www.scribeandcanvas.com
South Carolina

Printed in the United States of America

To all who endure the storms, seek the light and find healing in time.
This is for those whose prayers may feel unanswered
but whose hope remains steadfast.

The Poet's Prelude

Life often feels like a song—melodic, dissonant, and layered with meaning. Inspired by the soulful lyrics of *"A Christmas Winter Song,"* this collection of poetry is my response to the storms we weather, the questions we ask, and the healing we long for. Each section of this book represents a part of that journey—from the darkness of winter storms to the renewal of healing and the enduring belief that time, faith, and love can restore us. My hope is that these words will bring solace to those seeking light amidst their shadows.

Table of Contents

Winter Storms

"Through the fiercest storms,
we uncover the strength within."

The Hushed Land

Through icy winds that scour hills,
The land lies hushed, its breath – still.
The trees stand bare, branches groan,
While frost enshrines the earth as stone.

Yet even in this wintry plight,
The storm must bow to morning's light.
What frost now steals, spring will reclaim,
And life will rise from the pain.

Sky's Shattered Light

Beneath the storm, no stars appear;
The heavens weep of icy tears.
The world is veiled in winter's sigh,
As shadows stretch across the sky.

But storms are fleeting, skies must clear,
And hope can thrive in hearts sincere.
Though dark may reign, its time is brief,
For dawn must come and bring relief.

The Driftwood Dreams

On frozen seas, my dreams set sail,
Their paths obscured by winter's veil.
Each wave that crashes bends my will,
Yet drifting hearts find strength to still.

The frost may bite, the winds may tear,
Yet hope is boundless, light as air.
For even in the bleakest streams,
The driftwood cradles steadfast dreams.

December's Cry

December wails with mournful breath,
A lullaby of icy death.
Each snowflake falls, a fleeting prayer,
That melts in whispers on the air.

But seasons spin as fate commands,
Their clockwork turning nature's hands.
And winter's grief will soon decline,
As spring returns – winter's demise.

Frostbitten Prayers

I send my prayers on wings of frost,
Uncertain if they'll land, or lost.
The bitter gale bears no reply,
Yet still, my soul looks to the sky.

For faith, though trembling, still can stand,
A candle cupped by steady hands.
And even when the answer's slow,
I trust in seeds beneath the snow.

Frozen Faith

Encased in ice, my spirit waits,
Through frozen nights, through iron gates.
The stars are silent, clouds hang low,
Yet still, I feel a faintest glow.

For winter, cruel though it may seem,
Is but the shadow of a dream.
And dreams endure, though skies turn gray,
Till springtime brings a brighter day.

Snowful Whispers

The snow, it whispers as it falls,
Its hush a voice that softly calls.
It speaks of time, of fleeting grace,
Of moments lost we cannot chase.

Yet in its cold embrace, I find
A quiet healing, peace of mind.
For winter's song, though sharp and clear,
Prepares the soil for spring's premiere.

The Weight of Frost

The trees wear winter like an old regret,
their limbs heavy with frost,
bowing to a wind that remembers no mercy.

Each breath of air is sharp,
etching its way into lungs that
hunger for warmth.

The earth speaks softly in the silence,
its frozen skin hiding the roots
that still dream of spring.

Shards of Ice

The storm carves patterns on the glass,
A fleeting art of frost and pain.
What beauty lives, it will not last,
The fleeting cold cannot remain.

A fleeting art of frost and pain,
The wind's lament begins to fade.
The fleeting cold cannot remain,
For spring will rise to heal what's made.

The wind's lament begins to fade,
What beauty lives, it will not last.
For spring will rise to heal what's made,
The storm carves patterns on the glass.

Stillness Beneath the Snow

The snow descends in silence, veiling all,
A shroud of white where shadows used to dwell.
Beneath this stillness lies a hum of life,
The roots of trees, the sleeping seeds of spring.

Though cold may strip the world of color's blush,
It cannot stop the pulse that warms the soil.
For every winter holds within its heart,
The promise of an ending,
The promise of a dawn.

Winter's Cathedral

Hail to the solemn halls of winter,
where trees stand robed in frost,
their branches like silent arches,
reaching for a distant, unseen heaven.

The ground, a mosaic of ice and shadow,
creaks beneath each step.
The air is a hymn, low and mournful,
whispering truths too ancient to bear names.

Here, in this cathedral of stillness,
I bow not in despair, but in awe—
For even in its coldest season,
the earth is holy.

Fractures in the Cold

There are cracks in the ice,
splinters that zigzag like lightning
across the surface of a frozen lake.

The weight of the world bears down,
but even ice breaks
to let the water breathe again.

I trace those fractures with my eyes,
imagining the sound—
a distant echo of freedom waiting to erupt.

Snowbound Memories

Footsteps fade from view,
winter hides all that remains—
a quiet farewell.

The Frozen Watcher

The moon stands vigil, silver and still,
its gaze locked upon a world held captive.

Each shadow stretches longer, darker,
etching stories of a time before the freeze.

A figure moves—small, insignificant—
through the quiet chaos of the storm,
their breath clouding the air,
their heart clinging to the promise of warmth.

The watcher waits, silent, unblinking,
as if to say: Hold fast. Spring comes.

The Blizzard's Echoes

The wind cries out through empty, hollow halls,
Its voice a chorus, wild and unrestrained.
Each flake a whisper as it softly falls.

The trees stand sentinel, their frozen thralls,
Bound tight by winter's grip, their strength retained.
The wind cries out through empty, hollow halls.

I hear its song, a call that both appalls
And soothes, its power neither tamed nor feigned.
Each flake a whisper as it softly falls.

Though frost encases, life beneath it sprawls,
The seeds endure, though skies seem dimly stained.
The wind cries out through empty, hollow halls,
Each flake a whisper as it softly falls.

The Burden of Silence

Snow covers the earth like an unfinished story,
its pages blank, its edges frayed.
I tread softly, each step
an interruption in this fragile quiet.

The sky is a gray canvas,
painted with clouds too heavy to move.
I wonder how long the silence will hold—
whether it will crack beneath the weight
of waiting for a season that never comes.

Veins of Frost

Beneath the frost, the earth still breathes unseen,
Its veins of water trace a frozen line.
The roots, though buried, drink from depths serene,
Awaiting spring to heal the wounded vine.

The air is sharp; it cuts with winter's blade,
Yet beauty gleams within the icy face.
Each crystal shard, a fleeting world displayed,
A frozen song of nature's quiet grace.

Though winter claims the day with bitter hand,
It cannot hold the sun from finding all.
And when its rule dissolves like grains of sand,
The frozen tears of earth will cease to fall.

A Hearth's Cold Embers

The fire within has dwindled, left to ash,
Its embers choking on the icy air.
The hearth once roared, a beacon for the lost,
But now it shivers, waiting for the spark.

I sit beside it, hands outstretched in vain,
The chill within more biting than the frost.
Yet even ashes hold the seeds of flames;
The smallest breath can coax them back to life.

Winter's Songbird

A songbird perches on the edge of winter,
its voice a single thread of gold
woven through the tapestry of white.

Its melody is neither bold nor bright—
a fragile thing, soft as snow.

Still, it sings.
Through wind.
Through silence.
It sings.

And though its song is swallowed by the storm,
I hear it, faint but steady,
a promise stitched into the cold.

The Unyielding Leaf

One leaf clings to the branch,
its edges curled like fingers
grasping what little warmth remains.

It dances in the wind—
not with joy, but with defiance,
its fragile form refusing to yield.

Winter watches,
its breath frosting the earth below,
but the leaf persists,
holding its ground
until the storm passes.

Shadows of Faith

"Even in the deepest shadows,
faith lights our path."

Flickering Candle

The flame dances uncertain,
its light wavering against the pull of night.
I sit in its glow,
watching shadows rise and fall,
their shapes too familiar to dismiss,
too distant to hold.

Each flicker whispers, Do not trust the dark.
But the shadows, they sing:
Be ye all alone.

Still, the flame persists,
a fragile defiance
against the tide of doubt.

The Weight of an Unspoken Prayer

What words remain when silence takes its place,
When lips refuse to part in holy plea?
The heart still murmurs prayers without its voice,
Its rhythm marking hopes it cannot speak.

Though doubts entwine, their roots a tangled vine,
I feel a stirring where my faith has waned.
A quiet promise whispers in the void:
The weight of grace will lift what burdens me.

The Bridge of Belief

O faith, you are a bridge spanning the void,
Your planks carved from whispers and trust.

I tread lightly across your breadth,
each step a question: Will you hold?

Below, the chasm yawns—
a gulf of fear, of reason unkind.
Above, the stars shine faintly,
guiding my faltering feet.

You do not falter, though I shake.
You endure, though I waver.
faith, you are the path,
even when I cannot see.

Shadows Speak

They whisper when the light is low,
when doubt creeps in and certainty flees.

Their voices are not loud—
they don't need to be.
They thrive in the stillness,
in the cracks of unspoken fears.

But I have learned to answer back,
to name the shadows,
to remind them they are but shapes
cast by a greater light.

The Unseen Hand

How heavy feels the heart that cannot see
The hand that steadies when shadows fall.
Yet faith is not the art of clarity,
But trust what sustains and shields us all.

The stars may fade; and skies turn gray,
And doubt may rise as night eclipses noon.
Yet even in the darkest stretch of day,
A hand unseen cradles every tune.

So though I walk through valleys wrapped in shade,
And fear the weight of silence, sharp and near,
I place my trust in whispers softly made—
The voice of faith that breaks bonds of fear.

A Lament of Stars

The stars dim behind clouds too heavy to carry,
their light retreating like promises deferred.

I search the heavens,
but find only my own reflection
in the glassy expanse of doubt.

Still, I look.
Still, I wait.
Even a single star can guide a wanderer home.

The Quiet Answer

I asked my questions in the night,
The answers whispered soft and low.
Through shadows' depths, I sought the light,
But darkness lingered where I'd go.

The answers whispered soft and low,
A gentle hum beneath my fear.
Though darkness lingered where I'd go,
A quiet hope drew ever near.

A gentle hum beneath my fear,
Through shadows' depths, I sought the light.
A quiet hope drew ever near—
I asked my questions in the night.

When the Wind Stills

The tempest fades, its rage no longer felt,
Yet silence follows, vast and unrestrained.
What fills this quiet void? The soul now waits,
Suspended in the calm that grief has left.

I stand upon this fragile ground, unsure
If stillness heals or breaks the heart anew.
But faith, like roots, runs deep beneath the soil,
Its strength unseen but steady in the dark.

The Shadow's Edge

The shadow stretches long,
its edge sharp against the fading light.
I wonder where it ends,
if it ends.

The shadow moves with me,
silent, steady,
a companion I did not choose.

But shadows are born of light—
and light,
even faint,
endures.

The Space Between

The space between belief and doubt is wide,
A chasm where my trembling heart resides.
Each step I take, the ground feels less a guide.

The winds of fear and hope both coincide,
Their whispers pulling at my wavering strides.
The space between belief and doubt is wide.

Yet still I walk; my faith cannot subside,
Though trust, like fire, dims but never hides.
Each step I take, the ground feels less a guide.

For faith is forged where certainty's denied,
A fragile bridge that leads where peace abides.
The space between belief and doubt is wide;
Each step I take, the ground feels less a guide.

Beneath the Gaze of Still Waters

There is a quiet in still waters,
a depth that does not demand answers
but offers reflection.

I see myself in its surface,
both distorted and clear—
questions ripple,
but they do not break me.

The water holds its secrets gently,
inviting me to trust
what lies beneath.

Footsteps in the Dark

The path unseen is treacherous and cold,
Each step a gamble with uncertain ground.
Yet faintly, through the mist, I hear the sound
Of footsteps that have walked this way before.

I follow them, though doubt still grips my chest.
The darkness thickens; I cannot see clear.
Yet in each echo lies a truth profound:
I am not walking this path alone.

The Shadow's Hymn

O shadow, you who linger near,
What song do you sing in my fear?
Your voice a low and steady hum,
A cadence born when light succumbs.

You are no villain, no thief of joy,
But rather a herald I must employ.
For where you gather, light must play,
And through your presence, faith finds its way.

Doubt's Silence

Doubt does not shout.
It waits.
Silent.

It curls in the corners of thought,
settling in the spaces
where light has failed to reach.

It is the breath between prayers,
the pause in belief,
a shadow cast by fear.

But silence is not its victory.
It is merely a canvas
waiting to be painted
with trust.

A Thread of Hope

In darkness, threads of hope are sewn,
A fragile line to pull me near.
Though faith may waver, seeds are sown,
Their whispers blooming in my fear.

A fragile line to pull me near,
To bridges built on quiet trust.
Their whispers blooming in my fear,
A light that shines despite the dust.

To bridges built on quiet trust,
I walk with caution, yet I go.
A light that shines despite the dust,
In darkness, threads of hope are sewn.

The Hollowing

There is a hollow space within the soul,
A cavern carved by grief and fed by doubt.
Its walls, though dark, hold echoes of the whole,
A quiet place where faith might still break out.

The light seeps in through cracks too small to see,
A gentle glow that softens shadow's hand.
Though fear may whisper, You are lost to me,
The hollow knows the weight it cannot stand.

For faith requires a space to call its own,
A hollow heart where it can root and grow.
The shadow, though it claims the heart as stone,
Is but the soil where seeds of courage sow.

The Silence of Stars

Not every prayer receives an answer,
not every cry echoes back.
The silence of the stars is deafening,
a vastness that holds its tongue.

Yet I wonder—
is the silence itself a reply?
A reminder that light travels,
even when unseen?

The stars are not absent,
only distant.
And distance,
I've learned,
is not forever.

The Anchor and the Abyss

I am suspended in this storm of thought,
An anchor tied to depths I cannot see.
The weight pulls heavy; yet it keeps me still,
Prevents the abyss from swallowing me whole.

Each doubt a wave that crashes on my chest,
Yet every wave reminds me I am here.
For though the waters rise, I will not sink;
The anchor holds me fast against the tide.

A Whisper in the Void

In the void,
there is a whisper.
Soft, like the rustling of leaves,
gentle, like a memory
that has yet to fade.

It carries no answers,
only presence.
It does not promise light,
but it holds the dark at bay.

In the void,
a whisper is enough.

When Faith Rises

When faith arises in the quiet night,
It stirs the soul from restless, weary sleep.
A spark that blooms and sets the dark alight.

Though shadows linger, casting off their blight,
This fragile flame of trust will softly creep
When faith arises in the quiet night.

It reaches where no earthly hand takes flight,
Through chasms deep, and oceans cold and steep,
A spark that blooms and sets the dark alight.

And though the dawn may yet be far from sight,
The heart will hold the promise it must keep—
When faith arises in the quiet night,
A spark that blooms and sets the dark alight.

The Seasons Turn

"With each turn of the season,
hope springs anew."

Greens First Shoot

Beneath the frost,
the earth stirs quietly.
Its breath is slow, deliberate,
a whisper beneath winter's weight.

Then, the first green shoot—
bold, fragile,
defiant against the cold.

It rises,
not because the frost has fled,
but because it must.

A Song for Changing Leaves

The leaves do not regret their fall from grace,
Their brilliance only fleeting as they fade.
For even in decay, they write the tale
Of seasons past and those yet to arrive.

Their beauty, brief, still lingers in the mind,
A melody that echoes in the heart.
And though the trees will stand in naked grief,
They know the promise held in spring's embrace.

The River's Lesson

O river, you teach the art of letting go,
Your waters unbound, unyielding.

You do not resist the stones in your path,
but carve your way around them,
their edges softened by your persistence.

Teach me this grace,
to flow unbroken,
to turn when turning is necessary,
to trust the pull of the unseen sea.

The Edge of Winter

The edge of winter hums with whispered spring,
Though frost still bites and snowflakes fill the air.
The earth below begins remembering.

The wind, though cold, hints at a softer thing,
A gentle touch that's hidden, but it's there—
The edge of winter hums with whispered spring.

The silent buds prepare their blossoming,
The barren trees will soon no longer bear.
The earth below begins remembering.

And though the ice still clings to everything,
The warmth beneath begins to rise and share.
The edge of winter hums with whispered spring;
The earth below begins remembering.

Turning Toward the Sun

Even the smallest seed
knows when to turn its face
toward the sun.

It does not question the light,
does not demand assurance
of success or bloom.

It simply follows the pull—
a quiet instinct,
a turning toward warmth
even when the shadow lingers.

The Sky Remembers

The sky forgets its mourning clouds of gray,
Its tears dissolve into the warming air.
The sun, no longer veiled, resumes its course,
A steady hand that writes upon the earth.

What once was heavy yields to softer hues,
The blushing pink of dawn, the gold of dusk.
And in this palette, life begins anew,
A canvas vast and filled with endless skies.

In the Wake of Frost

The frost recedes, its touch grows light,
The earth begins to stretch and wake.
What once was hidden greets the sight,
And life returns where none could take.

The earth begins to stretch and wake,
The roots beneath uncoil, ascend.
And life returns where none could take,
A bloom that knows no bitter end.

The roots beneath uncoil, ascend,
What once was hidden greets the sight.
A bloom that knows no bitter end—
The frost recedes, its touch grows light.

Between Seasons

It is the in-between
that holds the most tension—
where the winds carry both chill and warmth,
where the ground is both hard and soft,
where the heart hesitates
between hope and retreat.

But here,
in this fragile balance,
is where growth begins.

A Softening World

The thaw begins in whispers, not in shouts,
The earth exhaling all its pent-up grief.
The streams resume their song, a gentle hymn,
Their waters tracing paths long locked by ice.

And though the land still bears its winter scars,
A softening begins within the soil.
The seasons turn as hearts begin to mend,
Each cycle one step closer to the bloom.

When Winds Shift

O shifting wind,
you who carry the scent of new beginnings,
tell me where you've been.

Have you touched the mountains,
felt the cold kiss of their snow,
or grazed the meadows
where green is still a memory?

You are neither here nor there,
but in your restlessness,
I find a promise—
that no season lasts forever.

A Break in the Clouds

A break in clouds reveals the light above,
Though fleeting, it restores the heart to peace.
A glimpse that speaks of grace, of boundless love.

The storm, though fierce, can never fully shove
The sun away, its strength cannot decrease.
A break in clouds reveals the light above.

Though shadows cling, the skies will rise above,
Their constant turning brings a sure release.
A glimpse that speaks of grace, of boundless love.

And in that moment, I can't help but shove
My doubt aside, let hope in me increase.
A break in clouds reveals the light above,
A glimpse that speaks of grace, of boundless love.

The Slow Return

Healing is never sudden.
It is the drip of melting snow,
the unfurling of a leaf.

It does not rush,
nor does it falter.
It simply moves forward,
carrying with it the wisdom of waiting.

The slow return reminds me:
time is not the enemy,
but the soil in which I grow.

Echoes of Seasons Past

The echoes of the season still persist,
A phantom chill that clings to air and bone.
Yet as I walk, I hear the softer notes—
A bird that sings despite the winter's hold.

The past does not dissolve; it lingers still,
But even in its grasp, the future calls.
For every shadow cast is born of light,
And every echo fades into the breeze.

When Spring Waits

Spring waits,
patient, deliberate.
It does not force its way
through the frost,
but lets the thaw unfold.

Spring waits,
watching the world
shift beneath its touch,
waiting for the right moment
to bloom.

Spring waits—
and so do I.

A Field Awakes

The barren field now stirs beneath the sky,
Its surface softening in thawing light.
What once lay dormant starts to testify,
Awakening to spring's impending might.

The seeds, long hidden, reach for air above,
Their fragile shoots a promise to the day.
Each stem and leaf declares the earth's deep love,
A gift renewed when shadows melt away.

Though winter's touch is felt in distant glades,
Its grasp recedes, the season gives way.
The field awakes, and with it, hope pervades,
A vibrant call to life's returning sway.

The Turning Path

The path ahead twists, bends—
its end unseen,
its stones unfamiliar.

But the turn is necessary.
Without it,
I would walk endlessly in circles,
lost to my own hesitation.

So I follow,
not because I know the way,
but because staying still
is no longer an option.

A Whisper of Green

The trees begin to stretch their brittle limbs,
Their bark softens beneath the warming air.
A whisper rises, faint, a shade of green,
A sign of life where death seemed to reign.

The leaves will come again, in time, in waves,
Each one a promise made and kept in faith.
And though the winds may howl and storms return,
The green remains, a whisper turned song.

The Call of the Swallow

O swallow, herald of the shifting skies,
You dart and dance with such relentless grace.
Your wings, though small, defy the storm's remains,
And in your call, I hear the promise: spring.

You do not linger where the cold still dwells,
But seek the warmth that pulls you ever forward.
Teach me your trust, your boldness in the face
Of all that turns and changes with the seasons.

The Snow's Last Breath

The snow surrenders softly to the sun,
Its glimmer fades beneath the growing heat.
The season turns; its end has now begun.

Each flake dissolves, its purpose now is done,
A quiet passing, beautiful, discreet.
The snow surrenders softly to the sun.

Its weight recedes, no longer holding none,
The earth breathes free beneath the thawing sheet.
The season turns; its end has now begun.

Though winter fades, its memory – spun,
A fleeting beauty never quite complete.
The snow surrenders softly to the sun,
The season turns; its end has now begun.

A World Reclaimed

What once lay buried rises.
The streams speak again,
their voices clear and unbroken.

The trees uncoil their arms,
welcoming light into their shadows.
The air carries the scent of earth,
raw, alive,
reclaiming its rhythm.

This is not a beginning—

Allow to Heal

"Healing begins where grace and time meet."

First Breath of Healing

Healing begins quietly –
a breath taken without pain,
a silence that doesn't weigh as much.

It does not arrive all at once,
but in fragments:
a word spoken,
a tear released,
a hand held.

Each moment a thread,
weaving the fabric of becoming whole.

Time's Gentle Hand

The clock does not rush forward in its steps,
Each tick a steady rhythm, calm, assured.
It understands the art of mending wounds,
The gentle touch of time upon the soul.

What's broken finds its edges softening,
The jagged shards no longer cut so deep.
And though the scars may linger on the skin,
They tell a tale of how the heart survived.

The Balm of Silence

O silence,
you who cradle the aching heart,
wrap your arms around my wearied mind.

In your stillness, I find
not emptiness,
but space—
a field where the soul can breathe.

Teach me to listen to your quiet song,
to trust the healing
in your unspoken words.

The Garden Grows Again

The garden grows again with tender care,
Though weeds have choked the soil of its breath.
Each root removed reveals what still is there,
A life beneath that has not met its death.

Though weeds have choked the soil of its breath,
The seeds of hope remain within the ground.
A life beneath that has not met its death,
With sunlight's touch, new beauty will be found.

The seeds of hope remain within the ground,
Each root removed reveals what still is there.
With sunlight's touch, new beauty will be found—
The garden grows again with tender care.

A Prayer for Forgiveness

Let me lay this burden down,
this weight that I have carried
far too long.

Let me loosen my grip on anger,
its edges cutting into my palms.
Let me offer the hurt
to the sky,
to the sea,
to the One who knows how to hold it.

Let me forgive,
not for the one who wronged me,
but for the heart that longs
to be free.

Fractured, But Whole

Though fractured, I remain a single piece,
Each scar a map of how I've come to heal.
What's broken does not mean the pain won't cease.

The shattered soul can still reclaim its peace,
Through time, through grace, through love's enduring seal.
Though fractured, I remain a single piece.

The cracks may show, but they will not decrease
The strength within; the wounds begin to heal.
What's broken does not mean the pain won't cease.

Each mark a testament of life's release,
The proof that even scars can make us feel.
Though fractured, I remain a single piece,
What's broken does not mean the pain won't cease.

The Weight of Letting Go

Letting go is not a light thing.
It is a weight,
the heaviness of what you carried
so long
it became part of you.

But when you place it down—
when you watch it settle,
unmoving, behind you—
the ground beneath your feet
feels firmer,
and the air ahead
clearer.

The Quiet Bloom

Healing is not loud.
It does not arrive with a shout
or fanfare.

It comes softly,
like a flower opening in shadow,
like the hush of dawn
before the world wakes.

It teaches me to honor the quiet—
to see the beauty
in what grows unseen.

A Place for the Broken

Not all that breaks can find a perfect mend,
But even shards can form a work of art.
The cracks allow the light to filter in,
Their jagged edges softened by the glow.

There is a place for all the broken things,
A refuge where the heart can rest and breathe.
What's damaged does not need to be erased—
Its presence tells a story all its own.

The Thread of Grace

A thread of grace runs through the tattered seams,
Binding the fabric worn by time and pain.
What once was torn is mended in our dreams,
Its strength renewed by love's enduring strain.

Binding the fabric worn by time and pain,
Each stitch becomes a symbol of repair.
Its strength renewed by love's enduring strain,
The tapestry of healing starts to flare.

Each stitch becomes a symbol of repair,
What once was torn is mended in our dreams.
The tapestry of healing starts to flare,
A thread of grace runs through the tattered seams.

When the Heart Begins Again

It doesn't happen all at once—
this reopening.
The heart is cautious,
learning to beat without fear.

Each moment a step:
a smile offered,
a laugh unguarded,
a hand reaching out.

These are the beginnings
of trust.
These are the signs
of life returning.

The Echoes of Kindness

O kindness,
you who move unseen yet felt,
how your touch transforms!

A word, a glance,
a hand extended in silence—
these are the echoes
that ripple through the soul.

You do not demand recognition,
yet your presence lingers,
a balm for the wounds
we cannot name.

Stay near,
gentle kindness,
and teach us
to heal one another.

A River's Course

A river bends but never stops its flow,
Its current steady, carving through the land.
It finds its way, no matter where it goes.

The rocks may try to stall its course, but no,
The river learns to weave, to understand.
A river bends but never stops its flow.

Its waters whisper secrets we should know:
The journey's strength lies not in what we planned.
It finds its way, no matter where it goes.

Through every twist, it carries on to show
That healing isn't something we demand.
A river bends but never stops its flow,
It finds its way, no matter where it goes.

The Weightless Soul

I did not know how heavy
my burdens were
until I set them down.

The ache in my shoulders
eased;
the tightness in my chest
gave way to air.

Now,
I float in the lightness
of letting go,
my soul weightless,
my heart unbound.

The Gift of Scars

These scars, once cursed, have grown to hold their worth,
A tapestry of strength upon my skin.
They speak of battles fought and lessons learned,
Of nights survived when darkness sought to win.

The pain they marked has long since found its peace,
Their presence now a symbol, not a stain.
For healing's gift is not erasing wounds,
But learning how to live and love again.

The Gentle Art of Rest

Rest is not a weakness.
It is the body's declaration,
the soul's quiet rebellion
against the tyranny of overdoing.

Rest is an art—
the way the breath slows,
the way the mind untangles.

In its stillness,
healing gathers strength,
a whisper turning into
a roar.

The Bridge to Wholeness

I walk a bridge that spans the space of grief,
Its planks unsteady, worn by years of storms.
Beneath, the waters churn with memory,
A tide of all I've lost and longed to find.

But on the other side, the ground is firm,
The soil rich with promise, soft with hope.
This bridge I cross is not the end of pain,
But where I learn to carry it with grace.

The Embrace of Time

The hands of time embrace the wounds we bear,
A quiet turning softens sharpest pain.
The marks we thought would last beyond repair
Begin to fade beneath its healing rain.

A quiet turning softens sharpest pain,
Its touch so gentle, steady, and unseen.
Begin to fade beneath its healing rain,
The scars transform into what might have been.

Its touch so gentle, steady, and unseen,
The marks we thought would last beyond repair
Begin to fade beneath its healing rain—
The hands of time embrace the wounds we bear.

Seeds Beneath the Snow

Beneath the weight of winter,
a seed waits.

It does not mourn the cold
or fear the frost.
It knows the thaw will come,
and with it,
a chance to grow.

The seed teaches me patience,
to trust in seasons unseen.
Healing, like growth,
cannot be rushed.

What I Leave Behind

O burdens,
how long you stayed,
nestled against my ribs,
whispering your weight into my days.

But today,
I leave you by the wayside.
You no longer fit
in the space I am creating.

What I carry now is lighter—
a memory of your lessons,
but not your pain.
I walk forward,
unencumbered,
free.

Beyond the Winter

"In time, all things find their place and peace returns."

The Shape of Peace

It isn't what I expected.
Peace does not arrive in grand gestures—
not in triumph or applause.

It comes in the small moments:
the first sip of tea on a quiet morning,
the warmth of sun on skin.

It shapes itself to fit the cracks,
filling spaces
Unknown to be empty.

A Journey's Rest

The path was long, yet worth each weary mile,
Each step a part of learning how to stand.
The peaks I climbed were steep but gave me strength,
The valleys deep yet taught me how to see.

Now at the journey's rest, I find my breath,
A space to honor all that came before.
For in the walk, I found not just my way,
But who I am, and who I'm meant to be.

The Clock Ticks On

The clock ticks on, its rhythm soft and slow,
A metronome for time's eternal stream.
It marks the moments we let come and go,
A gentle thread that weaves into a dream.

A metronome for time's eternal stream,
Its hands remind us nothing ever stays.
A gentle thread that weaves into a dream,
The past dissolves, and yet its echo plays.

Its hands remind us nothing ever stays,
The clock ticks on, its rhythm soft and slow.
The past dissolves, and yet its echo plays—
It marks the moments we let come and go.

A Song of Resilience

Sing, even when the world tells you not to.
Sing, though your voice cracks,
though your breath falters.

Your song is yours alone.
It rises from the depths of your being,
a defiant anthem
of all you have endured.

Let it echo,
not as a cry of sorrow,
but as a hymn of strength.

Fine in Time

We will be fine, though seasons bring their storms,
The winds may howl, but they will one day cease.
Within the chaos, healing starts to form.

The sun returns; its light will heal the norms,
Replacing shadows with a sense of peace.
We will be fine, though seasons bring their storms.

The heart adapts, it softens and transforms,
Its rhythm steadies as the doubts release.
Within the chaos, healing starts to form.

Though trials come, each spirit still performs,
Its strength revealed in how it finds its ease.
We will be fine, though seasons bring their storms,
Within the chaos, healing starts to form.

The Weight of Tomorrow

Tomorrow waits,
its edges sharp and bright,
its weight both promise and uncertainty.

I do not fear it now.
I have learned to carry its load
with shoulders fortified by yesterday.

The future bends
to those who walk toward it
with open hands.

The Language of Stillness

In stillness, there's a voice that speaks in calm,
A gentle rhythm humming in the void.
It does not shout or clamor to be heard;
It whispers truths too subtle for the day.

Its words uncoil the knots of weary thoughts,
A balm for wounds that once refused to heal.
In silence, I have learned the art of peace—
A space where time and soul are intertwined.

The Horizon Beckons

I see the line where sky meets earth—
not as a barrier,
but an invitation.

The horizon does not keep us in;
it calls us out.

Each step forward brings it closer,
yet it always remains ahead,
a reminder that the journey continues.

The Light Beyond the Storm

The light beyond the storm is soft, yet true,
A glow that spreads through skies once torn apart.
It whispers hope where darkness once it grew,
A healing touch upon a weary heart.

A glow that spreads through skies once torn apart,
It marks the end of struggle, loss, and fight.
A healing touch upon a weary heart,
The dawn returns to banish longest night.

It marks the end of struggle, loss, and fight,
It whispers hope where darkness once it grew.
The dawn returns to banish longest night—
The light beyond the storm is soft, yet true.

A Garden Reclaimed

Oh, garden once neglected,
how wild you grew in my absence.
Your paths overrun,
your blooms overtaken by thorns.

But I see the beauty in your chaos—
each flower that fought for sunlight,
each vine that climbed for life.

Now, I return with tender hands,
to prune and plant anew,
to shape what was abandoned
into something whole.

Echoes of Time

Time moves
in circular lines—
returning us to the places we left,
the lessons we thought we had learned.

Each echo carries a fragment of before,
a reminder
that healing is not the destination,
but rather the journey we walk again and again.

The First True Smile

It came unbidden, like a sudden breeze,
A lightness breaking through the heavy air.
My face remembers what my heart forgot—
The simple joy and pleasure of being.

No weight of yesterday could pull it down,
No fear of what tomorrow might yet bring.
This smile belongs to me and me alone,
A quiet testament to battles won.

The Dance of Healing

The dance of healing sways with steady grace,
A rhythm found in moments soft and kind.
It takes its steps within its chosen space.

Though stumbles mark the journey's fragile pace,
Its balance holds, a tethered peace defined.
The dance of healing sways with steady grace.

Each movement whispers love we must embrace,
A melody that lingers in the mind.
It takes its steps within its chosen space.

The heart aligns, its beats in quiet trace,
A harmony of soul and time combined.
The dance of healing sways with steady grace,
It takes its steps within its chosen space.

Where Rivers Lead

A river never asks where it must go;
it follows the path carved by time and stone,
always forward, always onward,
until it merges with the vast unknown.

I am learning to be like the river—
to trust the bends and turns,
the shallows and depths,
the rocks and bends,
the muck and miry leading on—
to the great journey's confluence.

The Quiet Bloom

No trumpet calls, no blinding light appears,
And yet, the moment comes—so soft, so sure.
The flower opens, petal after petal,
Unfolding to the world its hidden heart.

Its beauty isn't rushed or forced to grow;
It takes its time, as healing always does.
Each bloom a quiet hymn to life renewed,
Each breath a gentle vow to carry on.

Threads of the Eternal

The threads of life are woven, strong yet fine,
A tapestry of hope, of loss, of grace.
Each stitch a story, every strand aligned,
Its pattern flows through time, in endless space.

A tapestry of hope, of loss, of grace,
It shifts and changes, yet it still holds true.
Its pattern flows through time, in endless space,
Reflecting all that life has brought us through.

It shifts and changes, yet it still holds true,
Each stitch a story, every strand aligned.
Reflecting all that life has brought us through,
The threads of life are woven, strong yet fine.

The Light Within

Oh, light that lingers deep within,
how steady you burn, though shadows surround.
You are the fire, warmth unconsumed,
the glow that guides in the darkest hour.

Though I doubted your strength,
within my soul,
you never faltered.
You waited for me to see—
that I, too, am made of light.

Restored

The cracks remain,
but they are no longer flaws.
They are the places where light shines through,
where growth takes root,
where strength is born.

I am not who I was before,
and that is the miracle of it all.

When the Rain Stops

The rain will stop, though it may take its time.
Each drop a memory that finds its end.
The clouds will part; the sky will show its face,
A canvas painted blue with hints of gold.

And as the ground absorbs what fell before,
A life begins where none had dared to grow.
The rain may come again, but not the same—
Each storm a moment meant to shape the whole.

The Final Thread

The final thread completes the woven tale,
A piece of life, both fragile and profound.
Its colors glow, though muted in detail.

Each strand was placed with care, through joy and wail,
Its pattern shaped by love that knows no bound.
The final thread completes the woven tale.

A tapestry of heart and soul prevails,
A harmony in silence, full and sound.
Its colors glow, though muted in detail.

The work is done, its purpose to unveil
A life remade, a wholeness newly found.
The final thread completes the woven tale,
Its colors glow, though muted in detail.

Afterword

Life's journey is marked by seasons—times of struggle, doubt, healing, and triumph. This book was born from those moments, inspired by the moving lyrics of *A Christmas Winter Song* and the unwavering belief in hope, faith, and love.

To those who have walked with me through the winters of life, I owe a debt of gratitude. Your encouragement and understanding have been the warmth that carried me through. To my readers, thank you for opening your hearts to these poems and allowing them to become part of your own story.

May these words inspire you, comfort you, and remind you that no matter how fierce the storm, light will always follow the darkest days. Thank you for sharing in this journey.

www.ingramcontent.com/pod-product-compliance
Lightning Source LLC
Chambersburg PA
CBHW022142150726
47992CB00002B/713